Archery Book

learn how to archery in 90 minutes and pickup a new hobby!(including archery fundamentals)

Table of Contents

Introduction

I want to thank you for choosing this book, '*Archery*' and hope you find it informative and interesting.

Archery is a sport that has fed families, conquered civilizations and has also acted as a source of recreation for many people. Archery is both a sport and a martial art. As the former, it ranks with golf since it challenges the individual to develop a skill. As the latter, it helps to build control and self-confidence.

There are multiple manufacturers and models of archery equipment and there are many styles and forms of archery that have been developed around the two basic methods of shooting – either using or not using sights. Archery using mechanical sights relies on the accurate adjustment of the equipment paired to the appropriate distance of the archer from the target that must be shot. Archery without using a sight is dependent on the archer's instincts, where he or she must use a point-of-aim view to hit the target. Every archer must first develop his or her instincts when they begin archery since this method helps the archer maintain consistency and develop a good shooting form.

This book acts as a basic guide for both a beginner and an experienced archer. This guide does not cover all the information you would need to know to become an expert, but it contains information that can help you get started and improve your technique. Over the course of the book, you will gather information about archery, different equipment used by an archer and some techniques that you can follow.

I sincerely hope that both beginner and experienced archers gain some knowledge from the book. There are some common mistakes that have been listed in the book. Remember to practice as often as you can since practice does indeed make one perfect.

Thank you once again for choosing this book, good luck

Chapter One: An introduction to Archery

It is believed that the bow and arrow is one of the most important inventions in human history, right after the discovery of fire and the development of speech. There was a time when sticks and stones were the only weapons that man could use to protect himself from stronger, faster and bigger predators. However, when he was armed with a bow and arrow, he became an efficient hunter since he had the ability to shoot his prey and protect himself from predators.

The bow and arrow gave human beings greater protection, an abundant supply of raw material and a diet that was rich in protein. Early men believed that a bow and arrow were weapons that were crucial to their survival. Although guns replaced a bow and arrow over 500 years ago, archery is both a rewarding and unique challenge and has therefore evolved as a sport. There are at least six million archers in the world.

You can hear the twang of the bowstring at schools, club ranges, and municipal parks and in programs for numerous youth groups and the reasons for the increase in popularity of the sport are simple. Archery is a sport that can be practiced indoors, outdoors, with friends, alone and at any time of the year. The sport is inexpensive when compared to other sports, and archers have the chance to improve with age since skill and endurance are more important than brute force in this sport. There are some archers, aged 80, who have won competitions.

There were some primitive cave paintings that were discovered in Eastern Spain that proved that man has hunted with a bow and arrow for at least 13,000 years. Some ancient arrowheads found in Tunisia date back even further, and some of these arrowheads date back to 3500 BC.

By the 17th century in England, gunpowder and lead bullets had replaced the bow and arrow as a weapon. However, there were many trained archers and the interest in archery remained very strong. Festivals and fairs included some contests that captured the challenges and fun of archery. Many archers competed by shooting arrows through shields, shooting balls tossed into the air and shooting arrows over set distances. Tournaments were held and target archery became a competitive sport. The Toxophilite Society was formed in the year 1781.

Women had wanted to participate in archery competitions and the Royal British Bowmen became the first archery society that allowed females to participate in archery competitions. However, the British were not the only people interested in archery. Many countries in Asia and Europe included archery as a national sport. The Archery Guild was founded in the year 1453 in Turkey and this society introduced "flight" shooting and set aside large areas for the competition. Most competitors shot incredible distances that were recorded on stone markers. Sultan Selim recorded a distance of 972 yards and two inches in the year 1768, which was the furthest distance covered until recently. This record stood until the year 1968. Over the years, archery has evolved as one of the most challenging sports and is now included in the Olympics.

Archery Safety

Archery is one sport that takes pride in its safety record since it has the lowest number of injuries of all shooting sports and is considered the fourth safest sport of all sports. The reason for this safety is that the procedures and rules developed for archery must be adhered to by every participant thereby ensuring their safety. The Instructor, sometimes called the Range Officer, is the person who controls any shooting activity and archers must always obey the Officer's instructions.

Before you start archery, you must ensure that all articles of clothing are tied tightly to your body to avoid fouling. If you have long hair, you must tie it back for the same reason.

Archery is a fun sport. However, the fun often turns into a tragedy unless every participant adheres to the shooting rules. You must learn the rules and make it a point to follow them regardless of whether you are holding your bow or retrieving your arrows. You must remember that most accidents are caused due to the careless, thoughtless and callous attitude of the participants.

- Always follow the instructions of the Range Office.
- Pay attention to the commands and understand them before you make your move. If you do not understand a command, ask the Officer.
- Always use safety equipment, including the glove, finger tab and the arm guard. If your equipment is not positioned correctly the

Instructor may ask you to reposition your equipment. If the equipment has still not been positioned correctly, the Instructor will ask you if it would be alright for him or her to reposition that equipment for you.

- You must always inspect the equipment before you begin to shoot. If you have any damaged equipment, replace them immediately to avoid causing any injury. If the bowstring looks worn out, replace it immediately.
- Always use arrows that are the proper length for your bow since arrows that are too short often cause injuries.
- The clothes you wear must fit you snugly. Do not wear large earrings and tie your hair back to ensure that it does not distract you when you are shooting.
- Remove any pins in your chest pockets and avoid wearing necklaces that may hinder your aim.
- You must always have an arrow on the bowstring when you are shooting. If you shoot a bow without an arrow, you will damage the string when you shoot.
- Point and aim only at your target. When you have the target in your sight, draw the arrow and shoot.
- Ensure that you always aim and shoot at targets that are in the range. You have to ensure that you know what your target is and also make sure that it is safe for you to shoot. If you are unsure of the target, take a look, and if you are still unsure, do not shoot.
- You have to ensure that the area behind your target is clear before you release the arrow. If there is even the slightest chance that there may be someone behind your target, do not shoot since the arrow may ricochet off another surface or object and harm that person.
- When you have finished shooting, place the bow back in the rack and stand behind the waiting line. This action will help the other archers understand that you have finished shooting your arrows.
- You have to always walk and never run on the archery range since you may accidentally cross another archer, step on arrows on the

ground or trip or fall behind a target. You have to do your best to stay safe.

Archery Commands

The instructor, and sometimes archers, use the following commands during an archery session at the range.

Hold

This command is shouted when anybody on the range notices that there is a safety problem. When this command is made, every archer must stop shooting and remove the arrows from their bows. The commands "FAST" and "HOLD FAST" mean the same thing.

Come Down

Come Down is a command that is given to an archer. This command indicates that the archer must slowly undraw his or her bow and lower it until the arrow is pointing at the ground.

Archers to the Line

The Instructor gives this command to all the archers. When this command is said out loud, all the archers must take their place on the line.

Range Clear or Clear Down Range

This command is to ensure that nobody is present around the target. If you hear this command and find yourself in the range of the shooting line, make your presence known to the Instructor and move as fast as you can.

Nock when ready

This command is used when the archers are timed and means that the archer can place an arrow on the string, but cannot let it go.

Loose or Loose at Will

The instructor says this command to the archers in the range. This command indicates that it is safe for all archers to start shooting arrows.

Cease or Bows Down

This command indicates to the archers that they must stop shooting. They cannot draw any arrows once this command has been made.

Retrieve Arrows

This command indicates that it is safe for the archers to cross the shooting line and collect their arrows.

Archery Etiquette

The following are some points you must keep in mind when you are in the shooting range:

- Never distract an archer when he or she is shooting.
- Never remove or retrieve your arrows from the target unless the instructor has asked you to do so.
- Do not remove the arrows of another archer from the target unless you have asked them for their permission.
- Avoid touching an archer's equipment without his permission.
- Never shoot arrows into a target if you have not asked for permission from the Instructor.
- If you happen to damage an archer's equipment, offer to replace that equipment, even if they are arrows. However, if you damage an archer's arrow when you shoot at the same target, you do not have to replace it.
- Always thank the instructor at the end of the shoot.

Chapter Two: Archery Equipment

Now that we have covered the basic rules of archery, let us take a look at some of the equipment you must own.

Long Bow

The longbow is the most traditional type of bow and these are the bows you would have seen in the old Robin Hood movies. These bows were made from one piece of wood. The modern longbows are made from laminated strips of wood with a string and a leather-wrapped grip. Archers who prefer a traditional experience choose this bow over the other types of bows available. Since this piece of equipment is the most basic, it offers exciting challenges to an archer.

Olympic or Traditional Recurve Bows

One of the first evolutions of the bow is the recurve bow that is constructed with limbs that have curved built into them. If you own a bow that has a short limb, this curve will store more energy thereby increasing the speed of the arrow. A recurve bow can be made using machined aluminum or wood. This type of bow also provides a shelf where the arrow can rest which helps to improve the flight of the arrow. Archers who compete at national or international levels choose this type of a bow.

Compound Bow

The compound bow is one of the most technologically advanced types of bows. In this type of bow, an eccentric cam or pulley is mounted on each limb tip at the ends. Compound bows often have a let-off, which is a point on the bow that helps to reduce the weight of the bow between 60%-85%. This reduction in weight helps the archer remain at the full draw position for a longer period.

Arrows

It is not difficult to select arrows since it depends on the type of bow you are using and the target you are shooting at. You can choose from four types of arrows. Archers who use longbows often use cedar arrows. Archers using the compound or recurve bows often choose from fiberglass, aluminum/carbon composite and aluminum/carbon arrows depending on their needs.

Archery Accessories

Some accessories can be used to make things easier for you as an archer. A glove or finger-tab helps to protect your fingertips from being chafed when you draw the string back to let the arrow loose. An arm guard is worn on the arm that you hold the bow with to protect your forearm from being struck when you release the string. A quiver holds the arrows and hangs from your belt. You can also use a chest protector to hold back your clothing and also protect some part of your chest. If you use a compound bow, you can invest in a mechanical release. This device can be clipped to the D loop or string, and is used to nock and release the arrows instead of your fingers. When the bow is at full draw, you can press the trigger that will release the arrow.

Clothing

You must ensure that you wear clothing that suits your environment. If you are shooting in snow, ensure that you wear warm clothes and if the weather is warm, wear airy clothes. Regardless of the type of clothes you wear, you must ensure that no piece of your clothing can be caught by the string or the arrow. Remove or place necklaces under clothing and tie back any long hair. You must also remove any piercings you have may have that can get caught on the string. Also, remove any bracelets/watches from your bow arm. Ensure you wear appropriate footwear for the terrain and weather. Also, ensure you do not wear open footwear that leaves any flesh of your feet exposed as this could lead to injury from arrows in the ground.

Chapter Three: How to Shoot

Eye Dominance

Before you pick up a bow and arrow, you have to identify if you are left or right-handed archer. It is not necessary that a right-handed person will be a right-handed archer and the same can be said about a left-handed person. What is more important than identifying if you are a right handed or left-handed archer is whether you are right or left eye dominant. So, how do you identify this? There are multiple ways to do this, but most archers use the "Miles Test" method.

- Stretch your arms out in front of you.
- Place one hand over the other with your palms facing away from you and make a small triangle using your thumbs. Remember, the smaller the triangle, the better.
- Place a stationary object at a distance and look at that object through the triangle.
- Continue to stare at the object while you bring your hands closer to your face.
- The triangle will come to rest over one of your eyes, which is your dominant eye.

If you are left eye dominant, your hold the bow in your right hand and you draw the string back using the left hand. If you are right eye dominant, it is vice versa. You may be wondering why eye dominance is more important than hand dominance. Human beings rely on their dominant eye to identify the precise location of an object. Therefore, when you draw an arrow, you must ensure that you hold the arrow closest to your dominant eye. So, if you are left eye dominant, when you draw the string back with your left hand, this keeps the arrow closest to your dominant eye making it easy for you to look down the length of the arrow when you are aiming.

Bow Poundage

In simple terms, the bow poundage is a measure of how hard it is to draw the bow back. You must ensure that the bow is not too hard for you to draw. If it is, then you may be at a risk of injury. Most bows have the poundage written on them, which makes it easier for you.

Archery Stances

When you move your feet between shots, you tend to send arrows flying all over the place since you obstruct or change your aim. You must also mark where your feet must be to ensure that your feet are back in the same position. It is important to have a correct stance and this is one part that is often overlooked in archery. It helps to ensure that your weight is distributed evenly to make your shots more consistent. If you do not have the right stance, you will find it difficult to improve as an archer. Your stance is like the foundation of a building. Therefore, it must be correct.

There are four archery stances that are often used and your weight must be distributed evenly between both feet in all stances. You must place your feet shoulder width apart. Remember that not every stance will work for you and each stance has its own advantages and disadvantages.

Even Stance

The even or square stance is the one where your feet are in line with each other and in line with the center of the target. This stance is very easy and comes naturally to most archers. You can use this stance if you are shooting targets on even ground. However, you must use other stances if you are halfway up a hill or shooting from behind a tree since this stance will not provide you with balance when you are on uneven ground. If a person, especially a female, has a larger build, it will be difficult to shoot in this stance since it may impact your body.

Close Stance

In this stance, you must place one foot in front of the other based on your eye dominance. The close stance is one of the stances you can use if you are shooting on uneven ground. This stance often makes archers over-draw their bows. Like the even stance, the close stance also affects females with a larger build.

Open Stance

The open stance is the exact opposite of the close stance in the sense that the foot placed at the back is now in the front. This stance is good for uneven ground like the close stance and it does not make the archer over-draw his or her bow since there is a lot of clearance. The drawback to this stance is that the archer may use his or her arms instead of the back to draw their arrows. Archers with a smaller build may find it difficult to draw their arrows for longer shoots.

Oblique Stance

The oblique stance is like the open stance, except that in this stance the front foot is placed at an angle of 45 degrees to the target. This stance gives the archer good footing and good clearance to pull the string. It is difficult for an archer to maintain this position. Therefore, if you are a beginner, you will need to practice this stance until you have perfected it.

Gripping the Bow

Most archers believe that they do not have to worry about how they grip the bow. As stated earlier, it is important that you hold the bow in your right hand if you are right eye dominant and draw the string back using your left hand, and it is vice versa if you are right eye dominant.

Pick up the bow using the handle with your correct hand and place the centerline of the bow on your thumb muscle. Place your knuckles to the bow at 45 degrees and curl your fingertips around the bow. Your hand should maintain a relaxed grip on the bowl meaning that you must only grip it with enough force to ensure that the bow does not leave your hand when you release the string to shoot.

You should never let go or change your grip on the bow once you release the arrow unless it is for safety reasons. If you change your grip, you will change where the pile of arrows rests before they are released.

Nocking an Arrow

You must hold your arrow on the same side of the bow as your arm. If you hold the bow with your right hand, the arrow must be placed on the right side of the bow and vice versa. The arrow should have three fletching's which are attached at an angle of 120 degrees. One of these fletchings, called the cock fletching, is of a different color and must face away from the bow. This position will allow the arrow to slide past the bow without causing the arrow to go off on a course that was not intended.

If you shoot arrows where the fletchings are all the same color, you can identify the cock fletching by looking at the arrow from the back. On one side of the neck, you should have only one fletching while on the other side you will have two. The single fletching is called the cock fletching.

Gripping the String

Two modern ways have been developed to hold the string. The first method is to place three fingers below the nock of the arrow and all these fingers should curl around the string. This position will ensure that the string rests on the closest fingertip making it easy to shoot closer targets.

The second method, called the split release is where you place the index finger above the arrow nock and the second and third fingers below. This grip makes it easy for the archer to aim at targets that are at a great distance.

For both of these positions, you have to ensure that you do not twist the string or pinch the arrow. You can avoid this if you,
- Align the three fingers with the string
- Leave some gap between the arrow and your fingers
- Draw the string with an equal amount of pressure

Keep the rest of your hand as relaxed as possible and avoid contacting the string using your little finger or thumb.

You can use either an archery glove or tab for both grips. You have to also know that another way to grip the string is by using only two fingers. This grip is the same as the split grip except that you do not place your third finger on the string.

Anchoring the Arrow

The anchor point is where the hand that draws the string is pulled back to full draw. There are multiple places where the arrow can be drawn back. It is normally the face that an archer uses as the anchor point, and you must make sure that you draw back to the same point with every arrow. If you change your arrow, you change where your arrow will end up. There are three anchor points that a beginner can choose to use.

Cheekbone

The arrow should be anchored right below your eye and your index finger should lightly touch your cheekbone. This anchor point is great to use if you are shooting arrows for short distances, either five or ten yards. It also allows the archer to look down the full length of the arrow to find their aim quickly. If the arrow pile is being used for aiming, you must line the arrow with the bottom of the bow and loose the arrow. If the arrows are going low, you have to aim slightly higher. It is best to use either of the grips mentioned above, meaning you would need to use three fingers below the arrow.

Corner of mouth

The arrow should be anchored below your eye and the index finger should be placed at the corner of your mouth. This anchor point is good for medium distances. Since the corner of your mouth always remains in the same place, you can draw your arrow back consistently to your mouth without any trouble. Use the split release for distances greater than 30 yards and the three-finger release for distances between three and fifteen yards.

Under the Chin

This anchor point is where you must always use the split release and place your fingers below the jawline. This anchor point is great to use for long distances. When you release the arrow, the string should make light contact with your chin and nose if possible. Do not use this as an anchor point for close targets since you can overshoot your targets easily.

Now that you have got your grip and anchor point in mind, you can aim at your target and shoot.

Chapter Four: Precautions

People believe that they can handle a bow carelessly since it is not a firearm and cannot harm another human being. However, arrows, like guns, can be misused and cause harm to the archer or the people around him. Every archer has been slapped by his or her bowstring at least a few hundred times, and there are some cases where worse consequences have occurred. This chapter lists some points that you must keep in mind to avoid causing harm to yourself and to the people around you.

- The bowstring often breaks because of the torque in the bow. Therefore, the string must always be aligned with the cams. You must ensure that there are no twists in the string since the string can break and slap you across the arm and wrist. Be careful when you stretch the bowstring.
- Arrows should be flexed before they are released from your grip. If you have new carbon arrows, you must flex them before you release them. However, if the arrows are damaged or old, you should avoid flexing them since they could send splinters into the archer's face. There have been cases where broken arrows have pierced the skin of the archer.
- Always release the arrow well and ensure that you maintain proper stance. You must also ensure that you hold the bow correctly and draw the string only after you have made proper calculations depending on the arrow material, the string material, the bow poundage and the torque on the bow and string.
- You must ensure that you do not shoot straight up for obvious reasons. Remember that every object that is thrown upward comes down because of gravity. If you shoot an arrow upward, there are chances that it may hit you before you run away from your initial position.
- Never nock an arrow unless the Instructor has asked everyone to do so. You must also ensure that you only nock the arrow when you are at the shooting line.

- If you have dropped anything at the shooting line, do not try to retrieve it until the Instructor has asked people to put their bows down.
- As mentioned earlier, you must avoid dry-firing a bow. This action not only damages the bow and string, but also may hurt you.

Do not be foolish and try any new tricks if you have not mastered the basics of archery. You must know the environment, the archery range and the target before you shoot. This knowledge will help you keep yourself and other people safe.

Chapter Five: Frequently Asked Question

Why am I hitting my chest or arm?

This is a problem that most beginners face and there are multiple reasons why. The most common reason this happens is that of the incorrect grip of the bow. To make sure that your grip is correct, please go to the section in the previous chapter about the correct grip. If you still face this problem, you must check your stance.

Why is my bow often scraped by the arrows?

This situation often occurs when your bow is held too high or the anchor point is too low. You must ensure that you hold the bow right and the anchor point is at the appropriate position. Please check the sections above to ensure that your bow is held right and your anchor point is appropriate for your shooting distance.

Why do my arrows not shoot in the right direction?

If the arrows only go to one side of the target,

- You are using the wrong eye when you aim
- The arrows being used are not matched to the bow
- The arrow is not being released correctly
- You have selected the incorrect anchor point

The points mentioned above are only some reasons why the arrows are not going in the right direction.

Conclusion

Human beings have used a bow and arrow for centuries to hunt and protect themselves. Over the years, it has become a competitive sport and has also been included in the Olympics. Archery is a sport that instills a sense of confidence in the archer and is a skill that is worth developing.

This book provided you with information on what archery is and how it became the sport that it is today. You will also have gathered information on the different equipment you need to own to begin practicing. This book also provides information on how you should aim at the target and what you need to keep in mind.

Thank you for purchasing the book. I wish you luck on your new journey.

No sources used.